THOMAS EDISON

Reference Edition Published 1988

Published by Marshall Cavendish Corporation
147 West Merrick Road
Freeport, Long Island
N.Y.11520

Printed in Italy by New Interlitho, Milan.

© Marshall Cavendish Limited 1988
© Cherrytree Press Ltd 1988

Designed and produced by
AS Publishing

Library of Congress Cataloging-in-Publication Data

Thomas Edison.
        p. cm. — (Children of history; 6)
    Includes index.
    Summary: A biography concentrating on the childhood of the
inventor whose creations contributed to the comfort, convenience,
and entertainment of people all over the world.
    ISBN 0-86307-928-8. ISBN 0-86307-922-9 (set)
    1.Edison, Thomas A. (Thomas Alva), 1847-1931 — Childhood and
youth — Juvenile literature. 2. Inventors — United States — Biography —
    — Juvenile literature. [1. Edison, Thomas A. (Thomas Alva),
1847-1931 — Childhood and youth. 2. Inventors.] I. Series:
Children of history; v. 6.
TK140.E3T47 1988
621.3'092'4 — dc19
[B]
[92]

CHILDREN OF HISTORY

THOMAS EDISON

By Theodore Rowland-Entwistle
Illustrated by Tony Morris

MARSHALL CAVENDISH
NEW YORK, LONDON, TORONTO

The Great Inventor

When Edison was born, people lit their homes by gas, oil-lamps or candles. Trains and factories were powered by steam engines. There were no telephones, no moving pictures and no way of recording sound. Edison changed all that. Besides inventing the first electric light bulb (above) and the phonograph, he invented a vote recorder, an electric pen, a dictaphone, a speaking doll, and a way of preserving fruit. He improved the telephone, the typewriter, the stock ticker, electric generators and motion pictures.

Thomas Alva Edison was one of the greatest inventors who ever lived. He has been described as "the man who made the future" because he pioneered so many developments in modern technology. All together he patented (established a legal right to) 1,093 inventions, including the first sound recording device and the electric light bulb.

Edison's Family

The Edison family were descended from a Dutch family that settled in America in the 1730s. At first the Edisons were prosperous. One was a New York banker. But life was hard by the time Thomas Alva arrived on the scene in 1847.

Thomas's grandfather, John Edison, a Loyalist, took the British side in the American Revolution. When the United States became independent, John had to leave the country. He settled in Canada where his son Samuel was born in 1804.

His Father and Mother

Sam, Thomas's father, had a varied career. He worked as a carpenter and then as a tailor, before settling down as a tavern-keeper in a little town in Ontario. There he fell in love with an 18-year-old girl, Nancy Elliott, who was to become Thomas's mother. Nancy taught in the little local school. Her father was a Baptist minister. It must have caused a sensation when she married an innkeeper.

When a rebellion broke out in Canada in 1837 Sam decided he was not going to make the same mistake as his father. He sided with the rebels. But once again an Edison backed the wrong side – the revolt failed. Sam, hearing that he was about to be arrested, fled to the United States.

Thomas Alva Edison, seen here with his parents Sam and Nancy, was born on February 11, 1847 in Milan, Ohio. Their home is now a museum.

Born in the USA

Sam settled at Milan, Ohio, near Lake Erie, where he started a business selling timber and grain. He built a house, and then he was able to send for Nancy and their four children: Marion, William Pitt, Harriet and Carlile.

In three years Nancy had two more babies, and lost them both within a few months. Little Carlile also died when he was only six. So Nancy was overjoyed when her seventh child, a boy, was born. But she was worried, too, because he seemed very frail. His head was so big the local doctor thought he had something wrong with his brain. The Edisons named him Thomas after an uncle, and Alva after a great friend. As a boy he was always called "Al".

An Inquisitive Child

AN EARLY MEMORY
When Al was little, there were few railroads. People used to travel in covered wagons. Al always remembered seeing, when he was only three years old, a great collection of wagons gathered at Milan. These "prairie schooners", as they were called, were taking people West to prospect for gold, which had been discovered in California the year before. The wagons traveled in company, in "trains", because of the danger of attack by Indians.

All his life Alva experimented to test his theories. He would try one thing after another until he found something that worked. Trying to hatch the neighbor's geese was one of his early failures.

Most of the time Al played by himself. His sister Marion was grown-up and married, and he was 14 years younger than Harriet and 16 years younger than Pitt. He used to play outside the kitchen window where his mother could keep an eye on him.

An Early Experiment

Al was always getting into mischief. He was inquisitive. He constantly wanted to know things. He was forever asking questions, and trying things out. One day he asked why their neighbor's goose sat on her eggs.

"To make them hatch," his mother replied. She explained that the mother goose's warmth helped the eggs to hatch. Al said nothing, but he was thinking hard. Soon he vanished – and he did not come back for hours. His father went to look for him. There was Al, in the neighbor's barn, sitting on a clutch of eggs trying to hatch them. He wanted to test the theory for himself.

An Unexplained Silence

Al liked to watch the barges going by on the canal nearby, and whenever he could he visited his father's timberyard on the canal bank. One afternoon when he was about five he and a friend went swimming in a creek near the canal. The friend disappeared. Al waited for a long time, but the friend never reappeared. Al went home, but said nothing. In the middle of the night his parents woke him up and asked where his friend was. When Al explained that the boy had vanished, men went down to the creek and found him, drowned. Al was never able to explain why he said nothing about the matter.

6

More Mischief

Young Al went on getting into mischief. He fell in the canal and nearly drowned, like his friend. He fell into a grain elevator, and was nearly smothered by the grain. He went to places he had been forbidden to visit. Whenever he misbehaved he received a whipping, and a birch switch was kept behind the clock for that purpose. It was often in action.

A Public Whipping

One day he lit a small fire in his father's barn. The fire did not stay small, and the barn was burned down. This time his father took him out into the cobbled village square of Milan and gave him an extra-special whipping, in public. But Al was not punished harshly by the standards of the day, when parents followed the maxim "Spare the rod and spoil the child".

Sam Edison thought his son was stupid. "I can't make anything of him," he used to say. "He's always asking foolish questions." But Al's mother knew better. She had faith in her little son's ability.

Ruined by the Railroad

Soon the Edisons had to leave Milan. The townsfolk refused to have the new-fangled railroad through the town. They were happy with their canal and its trade. In 1853 the railroad opened – but it ran through the neighboring village of Norwalk. Milan lost its trade and its prosperity. Four out of every five people left the town. One of the first to go was Sam Edison, his business ruined. Al was only seven when they moved. The family packed up their belongings and journeyed, by carriage, train and paddle steamer, to Port Huron, Michigan.

The birch switch behind the clock was a powerful deterrent, but Alva's persistent curiosity still led him into innumerable scrapes.

A New Life

The town they moved to was a busy little port standing on the bank of the St. Clair River near where it entered Lake Huron. What was more, it was about to be linked by the Grand Trunk Railroad to the fast-growing city of Detroit, and by ferry to the Canadian part of the line on the eastern side of the St. Clair. The river forms the boundary between the United States and Canada. Sam rented a house, and put all his money into starting a new grain and timber business.

Moving to Port Huron was dispiriting for Mrs. Edison, but enormously exciting for Alva. He traveled on a train and a paddle steamer for the first time, and no doubt pestered their crews to show him the engines.

9

The Addled Schoolboy

Alva had only three months' schooling in the whole of his life, and that did not go well. It ended when the teacher said he was "addled". Alva ran home to his mother, and: "she brought me back to school and angrily told the teacher that he didn't know what he was talking about".

Soon after the Edisons settled in Port Huron Al had a bad case of scarlet fever. It took him time to recover, so it was not until he was eight years old that he went to school for the first time. The little school was run by a clergyman, the Reverend G. B. Engle, who believed in beating knowledge into his pupils. Al, who was as inquiring and difficult as ever, did not get on. He was at the bottom of the class.

One day Al overheard the teacher say he was "addled". In a temper, Al stormed out of school and marched off home.

When he told his mother she was equally angry. Next day mother and son went to the school. In no uncertain terms Nancy Edison told Mr. Engle what she thought of him. She said she would teach the boy herself.

Lessons with Mother

So lessons at home began. Nancy was a strict teacher. Every morning after her household chores were complete she taught young Al reading, writing and arithmetic. She read to him out of good books such as the works of William Shakespeare and the historian Edward Gibbon. Within a year Al was reading such books for himself. Nancy never managed to teach him to spell properly or to write grammatical English. Al only studied what he wanted to learn.

Al's Bedroom Laboratory

Thomas Alva was really inspired by one book, which his mother gave him when he was nine years old. It was a textbook on elementary science by a schoolteacher named Richard G. Parker. It was full of experiments that he could try out for himself. In this way Nancy Edison persuaded her son to study.

By the time he was ten, Al was spending all his spare time – and his pocket money – on chemistry and the materials for it. Al set up a laboratory in his bedroom, which quickly became a mess. There were bottles of dubious-looking chemicals everywhere.

Al was also experimenting with electricity. There was no central electricity in those days, so he had to use batteries. These were wet cell batteries, like those still used in cars. They contained the corrosive substance sulfuric acid, which damaged the furniture.

UP IN THE AIR
Life in Port Huron was not easy. Sam was having difficulty in making ends meet. He was full of schemes, but most of them ended in failure. One of his ventures was to build a wooden observation tower. Visitors to the little town were invited to climb the stairs to the top and peer through an old telescope at the spectacular view over Lake Huron. Sam charged 25 cents a time, and young Al used to collect the money. For a time, Sam did quite well with the tower. But after a time fewer visitors came, and the structure was allowed to fall down.

MARKET GARDEN
Buying chemicals and the
materials to build a better
telegraph set cost money,
and cash was not plentiful
in the Edison family. So Al
decided to earn money by
growing vegetables, helped
by Michael Oates. The
venture succeeded. Al
leased a horse and cart,
and drove around town
selling the vegetables. In
his first year he made
between $200 and $300.

Soon Al had more than 200 bottles and jars of chemicals.
He labeled them all "Poison" to prevent anyone else from
meddling with them. Nancy Edison banished them to the
basement. In his new laboratory Al spent many happy
hours experimenting. Some of his experiments were not
successful. He tried to generate static electricity by
attaching wires to the tails of two cats, and stroking their fur
vigorously. The cats produced no electricity, and protested
with their claws at this treatment.

A Human Balloon

On another occasion Al tried to make a human balloon, by
persuading Michael Oates, a boy who helped around the
Edison place, to take a huge dose of Seidlitz powders. These

powders give off gas and fizz when mixed in water. They are used as a laxative. They did not fill the unfortunate Michael with gas and make him float, as Al hoped. They made him very sick. Once again his mother brought the switch out to punish Al.

A Private Telegraph

As well as chemicals, Al experimented with model steam engines. But he was most interested in the electric telegraph. He built a simple transmitter and receiver from scrap metal, and ran a wire through the woods to the home of another friend, James Clancy. The wire was attached to trees. For insulators Al used the necks of old bottles, which he nailed to the trees.

Mrs. Edison taught Alva English, history, philosophy, mathematics and as much science as she could. Her son taught himself even more, with practical experiments such as this private telegraph, which would have worked well but for a stray cow that got caught up in the wire.

The Young Salesman

With amazing confidence for a boy of 12, Alva sold newspapers and confectionery on a daily 126-mile round trip on the railroad. Later he opened station shops for selling fresh vegetables and fruit, and employed other boys to help him.

In 1859 the railroad finally came to Port Huron. That meant the chance of a job for Thomas Alva. The job was as "news butcher", selling papers on the train between Port Huron and Detroit. Edison did not receive any pay for his work. Instead, he supplied the papers and kept the money from what he could sell. Better still, he was also allowed to be "candy butcher", selling sweets, peanuts and sandwiches on the same terms.

Sam Edison's business affairs were not going well, and the family needed another wage earner. Sam persuaded his wife that, though Al was only 12, he was not too young for this job. Many children of his age worked in those days.

Al had to get up very early, for the daily train left Port Huron at 7 in the morning. It arrived in Detroit three hours later, and waited there until 6.30 in the evening, when it started back to Port Huron. It was after 10 at night and usually dark before Al reached home.

Killing Time Usefully

The boy was alone in Detroit all day. But he did not waste his time there. Part of it he spent in the station telegraph office. He also visited local machine shops. In one he made friends with a young man named George Pullman, who was building the first of his luxury railroad cars. Al was allowed to sell fresh fruit and vegetables from the family garden on the train and at wayside stations, and he also sold some in Detroit.

The train's conductor, Alexander Stevenson, allowed young Edison to move his beloved laboratory into a spare corner of the baggage car, so he was able to carry on with his experiments while the train waited in the siding.

Pulled up by the Ears

One day Al was late boarding the train at a wayside station, where he had been selling papers. As it pulled out, young Al ran after it and made a grab for the rear step of the last car. Stevenson grabbed him by the ears and pulled him on board. Something seemed to snap inside Al's head. Soon afterwards he became deaf, though it is likely his deafness was due to an earlier illness. Years later, Edison wrote: "I haven't heard a bird sing since I was 12 years old." He reckoned being deaf helped him to concentrate.

Alva earned about $20 a week from his business. He used some of the money to buy chemicals and equipment for the laboratory which he was allowed to set up in the baggage compartment.

For "eight cents per month in advance", subscribers to *The Weekly Herald* could read, in Edison's own words, copy that "was so purely local that outside the cars and shops I don't suppose it interested a solitary human being". They could also read jokes like this: " 'Let me collect myself' as the man said when he was blown up by a powder mill."

The Young Newspaperman

In 1861 civil war broke out in the United States. It was between the Southern States, which supported slavery, and the Northern States, which opposed it. At first Edison took little notice of the war. Then he noticed that he sold his papers faster when they carried reports of battles. So he used to visit the offices of the *Detroit Free Press* to find out what the main story would be. Then he could decide how many papers to buy that day.

One day he heard that a huge battle had been fought at Shiloh, in Tennessee, with many casualties. Edison per-suaded the telegrapher at Detroit to wire a short account to stations along the line to Port Huron, and have it chalked up on bulletin boards. Then he persuaded the editor of the paper to let him have 1,500 copies of the paper on credit (he usually took 200). The papers sold like hot cakes, even though Al raised the price from 5 cents to 10 cents and – as his supplies began to run low – 25 cents.

His Own Paper

Al made $150 on this deal. With the money he bought a small hand printing press and some type, and installed them in the baggage car next to his laboratory. Soon he had taught himself to print, and began producing his own news sheet. He called it *The Weekly Herald*. It contained local news about the railroad and its staff, train and stage-coach timetables, For Sale notices, small ads and occasional jokes. Sometimes Al included war news if he learned it from the telegraph operators ahead of the regular newspapers. Al may have taught himself how to set type, but he still could not spell. The paper was full of errors such as "shure" for "sure" and "accommadation" for "accommodation".

In Deep Water – Again!

Unfortunately a friend persuaded Al to turn *The Weekly Herald* into a gossip paper, renamed *Paul Pry*. One of his paragraphs about a local man was too candid. The angry subject waylaid Edison and threw him into the river. *Paul Pry* ceased publication abruptly.

Al went back to his chemical experiments, but soon afterwards one of them went wrong and a fire started in the baggage car. The tolerant Alexander Stevenson thought that enough was enough. He threw all Al's laboratory and the now disused printing press off the baggage car.

So boring was Alva's newspaper "bantling", as he called it, that he had to print over 400 copies a week. George Stephenson, the British railway engineer, described it in a report to *The Times*. It was the "first paper to be printed on a train".

17

**As a result of the
laboratory fire, Alva was
thrown off the train.
Afterwards he had to make
do with selling newspapers
on station platforms along
the line. One day, while
waiting for the trains to
shunt, he saved the life of
the stationmaster's child, a
courageous act that was to
bring a change to his life.**

Al to the Rescue!

The train between Detroit and Port Huron carried freight as well as passengers. At some stations it used to wait for as much as half an hour while freight was unloaded or loaded, or freight cars were detached from the train.

One day the train was waiting at Mount Clemens station while some of the cars were shunted. Al sold some papers to the waiting passengers, and chatted to his friend the stationmaster, J. U. Mackenzie, who lived in a house by the track. He wandered off to look at the chickens in Mackenzie's yard. Then he turned around.

To his horror he saw Mackenzie's son Jimmy, who was not quite three years old, standing on the track throwing pebbles from the ballast. Behind Jimmy was a freight car, which had been shunted and was rolling down the track towards the train – and Jimmy.

Al did not hesitate. He threw down the papers he was carrying, and as his cap fell off he leaped down on to the track to snatch Jimmy to safety. The two rolled clear, landing face down on the stones.

A Reward in Kind

Al was the hero of the day. Mackenzie wanted to do something to thank him. But he was too poor to give Al a reward. Then he remembered that Al was always hanging around the telegraph office.

He said: "Al, you risked your life to save my child. I'll tell you what I'll do – I'll teach you telegraphing and give you dinner every day for three months."

Young Edison was delighted. He had always wanted to be a telegrapher. Fortunately he had the money he had made from his business deal with the newspapers, so he could afford to give up half of his route to another boy.

The Young Telegrapher

Alva worked hard as a telegrapher but still contrived to go on with his experiments. He would leave the telegraph key unattended and sneak off to the basement to work on experiments that he had read about in the latest scientific magazines.

Every day Al stopped off at Mount Clemens to practice telegraphy. Soon he was as good with the key, tapping out dots and dashes, as his teacher. And one day he turned up for his lessons with a fine set of telegraph instruments. He had built them himself in a friend's workshop in Detroit.

When his lessons in telegraphy were ended Al returned to Port Huron. A telegraph office had been set up in the town. The operator had gone off to join the Union armies in the Civil War, and Al was offered the vacant post.

Whenever he could he practiced taking down telegraph reports as they came over the wire. He often stayed up half the night to listen to the war news coming in at high speed to the local newspaper. Young Edison, now 16, found that his deafness did not prevent him from hearing the clicks of the telegraph, though it did cut him off from a lot of ordinary conversation.

A Good Idea and a Bad Idea

Edison's ingenuity came to the fore in the winter of 1864, when ice blocked the St. Clair River, cutting the telegraph cable and stopping the ferry that linked Port Huron with Sarnia, on the Canadian side. Edison used a locomotive whistle to signal in Morse to the Canadians.

This brought him a new job, as a night telegrapher at Stratford Junction, a station on the Canadian side. He soon got a severe reprimand. He had rigged up a clockwork device to signal at regular intervals that he was alert, while in fact he was having a quiet sleep!

A Runaway Train and a Runaway Al

A few weeks later he received an urgent message to stop a train. As he ran out to alert the signalman, the train ran past. Edison reported back, to learn to his horror that another train had been given the all-clear to come along the single-line track in the opposite direction.

Off he ran in the dark to try to catch the train and prevent the collision. He slipped, fell into a ditch and was knocked unconscious. Luckily the two drivers saw each other's lights and stopped. Edison was sent for and warned that he might face a term in jail. He did not wait to explain, but jumped a train which took him back to the United States, away from the threat of Canadian law.

THE BEST THING GOING
The telegraph was of key importance during the Civil War. Intelligence and field communications were speeded up enormously. Al realized how important it was when people mobbed him for his papers. He recalled later, "You can understand why it struck me then that the telegraph must be about the best thing going, for it was the telegraphic notices on the bulletin boards which had done the trick. I determined at once to become a telegraph operator." Thanks to his act of bravery in saving the Mackenzie child, his ambition was fulfilled sooner than he thought.

Five Wander Years

In Germany, years ago, apprentices used to spend a year traveling around to improve their skills. The Germans called this the "wander year". Edison had five "wander years". He became a "tramp telegraphist", moving from one ill-paid job to another in the American Mid-West.

Job Hopping

During this time he held at least 14 jobs, and was fired from each of them. Sometimes he lost his job for disobeying orders, and on one occasion for doing exactly what he was told. He was told to break into another message to send an important dispatch. He did. But the other message was being sent by the superintendent, who promptly fired him.

Edison lost other jobs because of his habit of rigging up home-made gadgets to save time or work. One device stored messages. It helped him and a colleague hide their lack of speed. They could receive the messages fast and send them on more slowly. Edison did not remain a slow operator for long. By the time he was 20 he was one of the fastest telegraphers in the Mid-West.

The First Electric Rat Trap

He was inventing more things now. In one place where he worked, the telegraph office was overrun with rats. Edison rigged up an electric trap which he called a "rat paralyzer". It did more than paralyze: it killed the rats.

Colorful Colleagues

He had many adventures, for his fellow operators were a rough, tough crew, and often got drunk. One night Edison, then based in Indianapolis, Indiana, was trying to relay an important war message from Washington, DC, to General

George H. Thomas at Nashville, Tennessee. The signal had to go through Louisville, Kentucky. But Louisville did not answer, though there were supposed to be three operators on duty there. Later it was discovered that one had fallen off his horse and broken a leg, one had been stabbed while gambling, and the third had gone to see a man hanged and missed his train back.

Two years later Edison himself was working in Louisville one night, when a fellow operator came in, roaring drunk, and wrecked the telegraph office. Edison calmly rigged up some temporary wiring to enable the work to go on.

Two insulated plates connected to a battery needed only a rat to complete the deadly circuit. Edison is said to have used this "rat paralyzer" to cure an infestation in the Western Union office in Cincinnati.

Home, and Away Again

In 1867 Edison returned home. He had ideas for many inventions, but no money to develop them. He found home a sad place. His mother was ill, and upset because the family were once again having to move from their comfortable home. Things, it seemed, could not be worse. He could not help his family; he was jobless and penniless.

A Lucky Break

Then a friend told him of a telegrapher's job with Western Union in Boston, Massachusetts. With the aid of a free pass from the railroad, for whom Edison had done some emergency work, he went East at a time when young Americans were being urged to go West to make their fortunes. It was a nightmare journey through heavy snowdrifts, and the train was four days late arriving.

In Boston people dressed smartly. Edison was tired from his journey, and wore shabby, baggy clothes and a wide-brimmed Western hat. The manager sensed that he was worth giving a break, and gave him the job, starting at 5:30 in the evening the same day. His fellow workers, however, were misled by his appearance and thought they would play a joke on him.

Answering the Challenge

They arranged for him to take copy from New York City. What they did not tell him was that the sender was one of the city's fastest telegraphists. Edison suspected that there was something afoot. But he was equal to anything the New York man could do – so much so that he even stopped to sharpen his pencil from time to time. Finally he broke into the flow of Morse with a message of his own: "Say, young man, send with the other foot."

When Edison presented his vote recorder to a Congressional Committee, they dismissed it for political not practical reasons. In the future, Edison vowed, he would only invent things that people really wanted.

A Waste of Time

Edison spent his spare time studying and experimenting. He noticed from the newspaper copy he took down that voting in Congress took a long time. So he devised and built a machine for recording votes automatically. The representatives simply pressed a "yes" or "no" button beside them, and their votes showed up on a dial.

He took the machine to Washington, DC, and demonstrated it to a committee of Congress. The committee chairman explained that they did not want to save time. During the long drawn out process of voting, people could be persuaded to change their vote.

AHEAD OF HIS TIME
Edison was ahead of his time with the voting machine. Only 24 years later, in 1892, the first voting machine went into use in New York State.

Today elections in many states are conducted with voting machines. They not only save time, but prevent errors in counting.

The Young Inventor

Edison gave up his job as a telegrapher to devote all his time to inventing. He turned his attention to the stock ticker, a device used to keep businessmen up to date with price changes on the Stock Exchange. It printed out the prices on a long paper tape. The machines in use were unreliable and kept breaking down. Edison produced an improved stock ticker that did not break down.

Edison made some money out of the stock ticker in Boston, but lost it all on a system for sending two different messages at the same time over one telegraph wire. Tests were a complete failure. Broke again, he decided to go to New York and try to get a job with Western Union, for whom he had worked as a telegrapher. But there were no vacancies. He had no money and nowhere to sleep.

In Edison's day, city prices were printed out on stock tickers. The name comes from the ticking noise that the type wheel makes as the paper tape passes under it. Edison's version of the ticker (above) printed words as well as figures, and did not break down. He opened an agency that relayed prices to more than 30 offices. Businessmen proved keener than politicians to take advantage of Edison's genius.

Striking Gold

At this point his luck turned. He applied for a job with the Laws Gold Reporting Company, which supplied a service of gold prices similar to that provided by the stock tickers. There was no job, but the chief engineer, Franklin Pope, allowed him to sleep in the company's cellar. A few days later the machine sending out the gold prices broke down. Edison, who was hanging around, soon found the trouble, and had the machine running again in two hours.

He was offered a job as assistant to Pope, and when Pope left to set up his own business a month later Edison took Pope's job. A little while later he joined Pope and another man in business. Edison promptly designed a new stock printer, made $5,000 on it, and set up on his own. General Marshall Lefferts, one of the heads of Western Union, engaged him to improve the company's own machines.

Will $40,000 Do?

Edison's work was so good that Lefferts called him into the office one day and told him the company wanted to pay him for all his improvements. "How much do you think they are worth?" he asked.

Edison thought he might ask $5,000, but said: "General, suppose you make me an offer."

"How would $40,000 strike you?" Lefferts asked.

Edison felt the room reeling around him. Slowly he said: "I think that would be fair."

Edison could hardly believe his ears when General Lefferts offered him $40,000 for his improvements, a small fortune in those days.

Edison demonstrated his light bulb in 1879. He "invented" it two years before but it took a long, painstaking search before he found a suitable material for the filament. In the end he used carbonized thread.

The Wizard of Menlo Park

Now that he was rich, Edison could afford to marry the girl he loved. She was named Mary Stilwell and she worked in his office. Typically, he proposed to her in Morse code, and nicknamed her Dot.

The $40,000 also enabled him to open his own workshop in Newark, New Jersey. Later he moved to Menlo Park, a village about 20 miles away. In the 11 years he was there he produced a string of important inventions. They earned him the nickname "The Wizard of Menlo Park".

His Greatest Inventions

One invention was the carbon transmitter, which made the telephone louder so that it was easy to hear. Edison's favorite invention was the phonograph. The first words ever recorded were "Mary had a little lamb".

Electric light was something people had been working on for many years. What Edison invented was the bulb, a small, cheap way of using electricity to produce light. Having done that he built a new and improved form of dynamo for generating electricity, and set up a company to supply power to part of New York City. It was quickly followed by other companies in Europe.

Edison made a fortune from his power companies, though there were times in the early days when he had difficulty in raising the money to pay his many employees.

Edison's most brilliant invention was the phonograph. Here, Mary Edison tries out the machine.

The Great Genius

Eventually Edison handed over the running of his businesses to other people, leaving himself time to experiment and invent. In 1889 he produced one of the first successful moving picture devices, the kinetoscope. And in 1914 he showed a picture on the screen which was linked to a phonograph – the first talking picture.

Another of his discoveries is known as "the Edison effect". This was that electricity was conducted between the hot wire inside an electric bulb and an independent cold wire. Unknowingly, Edison had invented the first vacuum tube or radio valve, the basis of modern electronics.

People used to call Edison a genius. Edison himself commented humbly: "Genius is 1 percent inspiration and 99 percent perspiration."

Edison and his second wife Mina at Menlo Park. Edison lived to the age of 84. In later years he is said to have worked on a device "so sensitive that if there is life after death it will pick up the evidence of it". No trace of such a machine has been found, but there is abundant evidence of Edison's genius all around us.

Important Events in Thomas Edison's Life

1804	Samuel Edison born at Digby, Nova Scotia
1810	Nancy Elliott born at Chenaugo County, New York
1828	Samuel marries Nancy Elliott
1829	Marion born
1831	William Pitt born
1833	Harriet born
1835	Carlile born
1840	Samuel II born (dies same year)
1841	Carlile dies
1844	Eliza born (dies same year)

1847	Thomas Alva Edison born, February 11th
1849	Marion marries
1853	Al tries to hatch eggs; fire and whipping
1854	Move to Port Huron
1855	Al goes to school
1856	Nancy Edison buys Al a chemistry book
1857	Al builds his first home laboratory
1859	Edison becomes "news butcher" on railroad
1861	Civil War breaks out
1862	Al starts *The Weekly Herald* Al saves Jimmy Mackenzie and learns telegraphy
1862-3	Al works in local telegraph office at Port Huron
1863	Al becomes rail telegraphist at Stratford Junction, Ontario
1863-8	Al returns to USA; roams as tramp telegraph operator during Civil War
1865	End of Civil War
1867	Al returns home
1868	Edison becomes a telegraph operator in Boston; perfects vote-recording machine
1869	To New York; becomes stock ticker supervisor; sells patents on his stock ticker for $40,000, and opens a workshop
1871	Edison marries Mary Stilwell Nancy Elliott Edison dies
1876	Edison moves to Menlo Park, New Jersey Alexander Bell invents the telephone
1877	Edison invents the phonograph and carbon transmitter for telephone
1879	Edison perfects electric lamp, October 21st Invents new dynamo
1882	Edison opens first commercial electric light station
1883	"Edison effect" patented
1884	Mary Edison dies
1886	Edison marries Mina Miller
1887	Edison moves to West Orange, New Jersey
1891	Edison patents his "kinetoscopic camera"
1912	Edison invents the kinetophonograph (talking pictures)
1915	Edison heads the US Naval Consulting Board
1917	The United States enters World War I
1920	Edison is awarded the Distinguished Service medal
1931	Edison dies, October 18th, aged 84

Index